Standard Grade | Credit

French

Leckie ✕ Leckie

© Scottish Qualifications Authority

All rights reserved. Copying prohibited. No part of this publication may be reproduced, stored in a retrieval system, or transmitted
in any form or by any means, electronic, mechanical, photocopying, recording or otherwise.

First exam published in 2004.
Published by Leckie & Leckie Ltd, 3rd Floor, 4 Queen Street, Edinburgh EH2 1JE
tel: 0131 220 6831 fax: 0131 225 9987 enquiries@leckieandleckie.co.uk www.leckieandleckie.co.uk

ISBN 978-1-84372-631-9

A CIP Catalogue record for this book is available from the British Library.

Leckie & Leckie is a division of Huveaux plc.

Leckie & Leckie is grateful to the copyright holders, as credited at the back of the book, for permission to use their material.
Every effort has been made to trace the copyright holders and to obtain their permission for the use of copyright material.
Leckie & Leckie will gladly receive information enabling them to rectify any error or omission in subsequent editions.

2004 | Credit

[BLANK PAGE]

FOR OFFICIAL USE

C

Total

1000/403

NATIONAL
QUALIFICATIONS
2004

TUESDAY, 11 MAY
11.10 AM – 12.10 PM

FRENCH
STANDARD GRADE
Credit Level
Reading

Fill in these boxes and read what is printed below.

Full name of centre

Town

Forename(s)

Surname

Date of birth
Day Month Year

Scottish candidate number

Number of seat

When you are told to do so, open your paper and write your answers **in English** in the spaces provided.

You may use a French dictionary.

Before leaving the examination room you must give this book to the invigilator. If you do not, you may lose all the marks for this paper.

SCOTTISH
QUALIFICATIONS
AUTHORITY ©

DO NO
WRITE
THI
MARG

Marks

1. You read this article about the French police.

Les policiers en ont assez!

D'habitude, les policiers vont aux manifestations pour surveiller les défilés, mais cette fois, ce sont *eux* qui ont manifesté les 10 et 17 novembre à Paris pour exprimer leur colère. Et pourquoi?

Eh bien, depuis le début de l'année, sept policiers ont été tués en France alors qu'ils exerçaient leur métier. Par exemple, au mois d'avril, deux agents essaient d'appréhender un cambrioleur dans le Val-de-Marne et sont assassinés. Et, au mois d'octobre, deux autres sont grièvement blessés quand ils arrêtent une voiture à Saint-Ouen, près de Paris. Au lieu de présenter ses papiers, l'automobiliste sort un pistolet et tire sur les agents.

(*a*) What did French policemen do on 10th and 17th November?

1

_____

(*b*) What happened in the incident in April? Mention **two** things.

2

_____

_____

(*c*) Two policemen were seriously injured in Saint-Ouen in October. What happened? Mention **two** things.

2

_____

_____

_____

Marks

2. The article about the police continues.

> "Ça suffit!" disent les policiers, et ils demandent une solution.
>
> Le gouvernement a promis de recruter 3000 agents supplémentaires pour renforcer les troupes. En plus, on distribuera des gilets pare-balles pour protéger tous les agents qui travaillent dans la rue. Les hommes politiques savent bien que l'opinion publique est avec les forces de l'ordre!

(a) What has the government promised to do to help the police?
Mention **two** things.

2

_____

_____

(b) Why is the government taking this action?

1

_____

[Turn over

Page three

DO NC
WRITE
THIS
MARG

Marks

3. You read this article about a possible new airport for Paris.

Un aéroport de plus pour Paris?

Paris aura un troisième aéroport, après ceux d'Orly et de Roissy. Des sept sites possibles, c'est celui de Chaulnes, en Picardie, qui a été sélectionné. Selon les experts, cet endroit a le maximum d'avantages.

Situé à 125 kilomètres de Paris, il est relié à la capitale par l'autoroute et un Train à Grande Vitesse. Comme c'est une région peu peuplée, le survol des avions ne gênera pas trop de monde. C'est un avantage.

Mais le projet provoque beaucoup de crainte chez les habitants de la région. Ils estiment que le gouvernement a imposé son choix sans véritable discussion, et ils ne veulent pas subir le bruit et la pollution que le projet leur apportera.

(*a*) What transport links with Paris does the new site at Chaulnes, in Picardy, have?　　2

_____

_____

(*b*) What other advantage does the area have? Mention any **one** thing.　　1

_____

(*c*) Why are the local people opposed to the new airport? Mention **two** things.　　2

_____

_____

Marks

4. The article about the new airport goes on.

Et pourquoi, disent les habitants de la région, un nouvel aéroport, quand ceux de Roissy et d'Orly ne fonctionnent qu'à la moitié de leur capacité?

Mais la construction de l'aéroport va prendre une dizaine d'années, et les experts disent que, entre-temps, le nombre de passagers va doubler – une augmentation que Roissy et Orly seront incapables d'absorber.

(*a*) Why do local people say the new airport is not required?

1

_____

_____

(*b*) How long will construction of the airport take?

1

_____

(*c*) How is the new airport justified by the experts? Mention **two** things.

2

_____

_____

[Turn over

5. You read this article about children who have to work.

Les enfants travailleurs

– des solutions difficiles.

Le 12 juin, l'Organisation Internationale du Travail (OIT) s'est réunie à Genève, en Suisse. Son but était d'alerter le monde au sujet des millions d'enfants qui travaillent. Ils sont 211 millions. Les plus nombreux vivent en Asie et dans le Pacifique.

Ces enfants doivent travailler pour aider leur famille. Sept sur dix sont employés dans des exploitations agricoles. Ils récoltent le tabac et le cacao.

(*a*) What was the purpose of the meeting held by OIT on 12th June?   **1**

_____

(*b*) Why are Asia and the Pacific countries mentioned?   **1**

_____

(*c*) Why do so many children have to work?   **1**

_____

(*d*) What do they do? Mention any **one** thing.   **1**

_____

Marks

6. The article about working children goes on.

Qui plus est, environ 10 millions sont employés dans les pays en voie de développement par les grandes entreprises internationales qui préfèrent engager des enfants puisque leurs salaires sont, bien sûr, moins élevés que ceux des adultes. Ces enfants fabriquent des habits, des chaussures, des tapis.

Grâce à des images chocs, qui ont fait le tour du monde, quelques entreprises ont voulu se présenter plus favorablement. Elles ont adopté un code de conduite, et elles n'emploient plus d'enfants. Mais le problème est difficile à régler. Si les enfants ne travaillent plus, que vont faire les familles qui dépendent de l'argent qu'ils gagnent? Ils risquent tous de mourir de faim.

(*a*) In which countries do many international companies employ children?

1

_____

(*b*) Why is this?

1

_____

(*c*) What do these children do?

1

_____

(*d*) What have these international companies now agreed to do?

1

_____

(*e*) Why might this not bring a solution to the problem?

1

_____

Total (26)

[*END OF QUESTION PAPER*]

[BLANK PAGE]

C

1000/409

NATIONAL
QUALIFICATIONS
2004

TUESDAY, 11 MAY
2.30 PM – 3.00 PM
(APPROX)

FRENCH
STANDARD GRADE
Credit Level
Listening Transcript

This paper must not be seen by any candidate.

The material overleaf is provided for use in an emergency only (eg the recording or equipment proving faulty) or where permission has been given in advance by SQA for the material to be read to candidates with special needs. The material must be read exactly as printed.

THB 1000/409 6/1030

SCOTTISH
QUALIFICATIONS
AUTHORITY

©

Transcript—Credit Level

> **Instructions to reader(s):**
>
> For each item, read the English **once,** then read the French **three times,** with an interval of 5 seconds between the readings. On completion of the third reading, pause for the length of time indicated in brackets after each item, to allow the candidates to write their answers.
>
> Where special arrangements have been agreed in advance to allow the reading of the material, those sections marked **(f)** should be read by a female speaker and those marked **(m)** by a male: those sections marked **(t)** should be read by the teacher.

(t) You are on holiday in France. You meet a young French girl called Nathalie.

(m) or **Tu passes des vacances en France. Tu fais la connaissance d'une jeune Française,
(f)** **Nathalie.**

(t) Question number one.

She tells you about her early life. What does she say? Mention any **two** things.

(f) **Moi, je suis née à Paris mais j'ai passé les sept premières années de ma vie en Algérie car mon père était diplomate.**

(40 seconds)

(t) Question number two.

She tells you about her family. What does she say? Mention any **one** thing.

(f) **Je suis la plus jeune de la famille. J'ai deux frères aînés. Ils sont plus âgés que moi de sept et neuf ans.**

(40 seconds)

(t) Question number three.

The family moved to Quebec in Canada. What difficulties did she experience there? Mention any **two** things.

(f) **En dix-neuf cent quatre-vingt-seize on a déménagé au Canada où on parle anglais et français. Au début, j'ai eu des difficultés à parler anglais et l'accent français était difficile à comprendre. En plus, ce n'était pas facile de se faire des amis.**

(40 seconds)

(t) Question number four.

She tells you what she liked best about her time in Canada. What did she like best about her time there? What does she say about where she went? Mention any **two** things.

(f) **Ce que j'aimais le plus, c'était les grandes vacances. Pendant un mois entier, on partait dans les vastes forêts; mon père louait une cabane au bord d'un lac à deux cents kilomètres de Québec.**

(40 seconds)

(t) Question number five.

She goes on to tell you more about this place. What does she say about it? Mention any **two** things.

(f) **Dans le petit village près de la cabane, tout le monde se connaissait bien. Il y avait des jeunes de mon âge et j'ai vite perfectionné mon anglais.**

(40 seconds)

(t) Question number six.

She tells you about how she spent some of her free time in Canada. What does she say? Why did she have to give up this activity?

(f) **Dans presque toutes les villes au Canada, il y a une patinoire et c'est là où j'ai appris à faire du patin à glace. Ça m'a vraiment passionnée. Malheureusement, à l'âge de treize ans, je me suis cassé la jambe et maintenant je ne peux plus patiner.**

(40 seconds)

(t) Question number seven.

Why does Nathalie not consider France her home? Which **two** family events does she refer to?

(f) **Naturellement je suis française mais avant l'âge de seize ans, j'ai passé très peu de temps ici. Quand j'étais petite, j'ai visité la France seulement deux fois; une fois pour le mariage de mon cousin et puis il y a cinq ans quand mon grand-père est mort.**

(40 seconds)

(t) Question number eight.

She tells you about her family now. What information does she give? Mention any **two** things.

(f) **Mes parents sont retournés en France il y a deux ans et mon père travaille dans un bureau dans la banlieue parisienne. Mes deux frères vivent toujours au Canada.**

(40 seconds)

(t) Question number nine.

What further information does Nathalie give about her family? Mention **two** things.

(f) **Un de mes frères est marié avec trois enfants, et l'autre n'a pas d'emploi en ce moment; il est au chômage.**

(40 seconds)

[Turn over for Questions 10 to 12 on *Page four*

(t) **Question number ten.**

One evening, you and Nathalie are listening to a radio phone-in programme. A French boy called Philippe asks a doctor for some advice.

What information does Philippe give about his eating habits? Mention **two** things. Why are his parents worried? Mention any **one** thing.

(m) **Tous les jours, je mange à la cantine de mon collège et je vais deux ou trois fois par semaine au fastfood. Mes parents me disent que je risque d'avoir des problèmes de santé à l'avenir, parce que je ne mange pas bien.**

(40 seconds)

(t) **Question number eleven.**

What does the doctor say about staying healthy? Mention any **one** thing.

(m) or (f) **Être en bonne santé n'est pas seulement une question de nourriture. Le corps humain fonctionne au maximum quand on mange bien et quand on fait régulièrement de l'exercice physique.**

(40 seconds)

(t) **Question number twelve.**

What does the doctor recommend in order to stay fit? Mention any **two** things.

(m) or (f) **Alors, comment rester en forme? D'abord, aller à l'école à pied au lieu d'y aller en voiture avec papa. Et puis, aller au gymnase pour faire de l'exercice physique est moins pénible si tu le fais en groupe, avec des copains par exemple. Finalement, quand tu dois faire des courses pour ta mère, pourquoi pas y aller en vélo?**

(40 seconds)

(t) **End of test.**

Now look over your answers.

[END OF TRANSCRIPT]

FOR OFFICIAL USE

C

Total Marks

1000/408

NATIONAL QUALIFICATIONS 2004

TUESDAY, 11 MAY 2.30 PM – 3.00 PM (APPROX)

FRENCH
STANDARD GRADE
Credit Level
Listening

Fill in these boxes and read what is printed below.

Full name of centre

Town

Forename(s)

Surname

Date of birth

Day Month Year   Scottish candidate number   Number of seat

When you are told to do so, open your paper.

You will hear a number of short items in French. You will hear each item three times, then you will have time to write your answer.

Write your answers, **in English**, in this book, in the appropriate spaces.

You may take notes as you are listening to the French, but only in this paper.

You may **not** use a French dictionary.

You are not allowed to leave the examination room until the end of the test.

Before leaving the examination room you must give this book to the invigilator. If you do not, you may lose all the marks for this paper.

SCOTTISH
QUALIFICATIONS
AUTHORITY

Marks

You are on holiday in France. You meet a young French girl called Nathalie.

Tu passes des vacances en France.   Tu fais la connaissance d'une jeune Française, Nathalie.

1. She tells you about her early life. What does she say? Mention any **two** things.

2

_____

_____

*   *   *   *   *

2. She tells you about her family. What does she say? Mention any **one** thing.

1

_____

_____

*   *   *   *   *

3. The family moved to Quebec in Canada.   What difficulties did she experience there? Mention any **two** things.

2

_____

_____

*   *   *   *   *

4. She tells you what she liked best about her time in Canada.

(*a*) What did she like best about her time there?

1

_____

(*b*) What does she say about where she went? Mention any **two** things.

2

_____

_____

*   *   *   *   *

Marks

5. She goes on to tell you more about this place. What does she say about it? Mention any **two** things.

2

_____

_____

*   *   *   *   *

6. She tells you about how she spent some of her free time in Canada.

(*a*)   What does she say?

1

_____

(*b*)   Why did she have to give up this activity?

1

_____

_____

*   *   *   *   *

7. (*a*)   Why does Nathalie not consider France her home?

1

_____

(*b*)   Which **two** family events does she refer to?

2

_____

_____

*   *   *   *   *

8. She tells you about her family now. What information does she give? Mention any **two** things.

2

_____

_____

*   *   *   *   *

[Turn over for Questions 9 to 12 on *Page four*

Marks

9. What further information does Nathalie give about her family? Mention **two** things.

2

_____

_____

*   *   *   *   *

10. One evening, you and Nathalie are listening to a radio phone-in programme. A French boy called Philippe asks a doctor for some advice.

(*a*) What information does Philippe give about his eating habits? Mention **two** things.

2

_____

_____

(*b*) Why are his parents worried? Mention any **one** thing.

1

_____

*   *   *   *   *

11. What does the doctor say about staying healthy? Mention any **one** thing.

1

_____

*   *   *   *   *

12. What does the doctor recommend in order to stay fit? Mention any **two** things.

2

_____

_____

*   *   *   *   *

Total (25)

[END OF QUESTION PAPER]

[BLANK PAGE]

FOR OFFICIAL USE

C

Total

1000/403

NATIONAL
QUALIFICATIONS
2005

TUESDAY, 10 MAY
11.10 AM – 12.10 PM

FRENCH
STANDARD GRADE
Credit Level
Reading

Fill in these boxes and read what is printed below.

Full name of centre

Town

Forename(s)

Surname

Date of birth
Day Month Year

Scottish candidate number

Number of seat

When you are told to do so, open your paper and write your answers **in English** in the spaces provided.

You may use a French dictionary.

Before leaving the examination room you must give this book to the invigilator. If you do not, you may lose all the marks for this paper.

SCOTTISH
QUALIFICATIONS
AUTHORITY

You are reading a French magazine.

1. You read an article about mobile phones.

LES TÉLÉPHONES PORTABLES... JUSTE *POUR LA FRIME? VOICI QUELQUES OPINIONS.

Les téléphones portables, ça sert vraiment. Mes parents en ont un chacun et je peux les appeler n'importe quand - par exemple, si je suis malade au collège.

Georges, 13 ans

En classe de maths, un téléphone a sonné. Le prof était vraiment en colère et il l'a confisqué. Mais il y en avait encore une dizaine . . .

Je trouve que chez certains élèves, c'est un peu de la frime.

Sarah, 15 ans

Quand on lit un magazine dans le bus et qu'on les entend sonner, j'ai envie de les casser. Après tout, on se débrouillait sans problème avant les téléphones portables.

Vanessa, 14 ans

Les portables, c'est super! Depuis que j'en ai un, j'ai plus de liberté: le weekend, je peux aller en ville tout seul, et j'ai la permission de minuit. Dans quelques années, avoir un portable, ce sera aussi naturel que d'avoir un walkman.

Pierre, 13 ans

C'est une invention utile, je l'admets. Mais au collège, c'est complètement ridicule! Il y a certains élèves qui l'utilisent pour parler à un ami qui est à vingt mètres d'eux. Ça, c'est de la frime et ils me font rire!

Jean-Luc, 15 ans

*pour la frime = for show

Marks

1. (continued)

Complete the sentences.

5

Georges: I can call my parents _____ .

Sarah: The maths teacher confiscated one but _____

_____ .

Vanessa: When phones ring on the bus I feel like _____ .

Pierre: At the weekend I can _____ .

Jean-Luc: Some pupils use them to speak to friends who _____

_____ .

[Turn over

DO NOT
WRITE II
THIS
MARGIN

Marks

2. You read an article about journalists.

Journaliste: un métier à risque

Les journalistes ne sont pas toujours libres d'écrire et de dire ce qu'ils veulent. Parfois des journalistes sont tués, emprisonnés ou victimes de violence. Une organisation, *Reporters sans Frontières*, s'occupe de les défendre.

En 2003 il y a eu moins de journalistes tués qu'en 2002, vingt-cinq en tout. Par contre, les agressions et les violences ont été plus nombreuses, et il reste encore cent dix-huit journalistes emprisonnés. Selon un rapport de *Reporters sans Frontières*, la majorité des journalistes tués ont été assassinés par des groupes armés. Et des gouvernements aussi sont souvent responsables de la mort de certains journalistes.

(a) What restriction is sometimes placed on reporters?

1

_____

_____

(b) What facts are we told about incidents in 2003 regarding journalists? Mention any **two** things.

2

_____

_____

(c) Journalists are being killed all over the world. Which **two** groups are responsible for this?

2

_____

_____

Marks

3. The article continues.

Pour la liberté de la presse

Les journalistes sont aussi censurés: il leur est interdit d'écrire certaines choses qui pourraient gêner le gouvernement d'un pays par exemple. Il y a plusieurs années, cette censure était surtout pratiquée en Chine, en Turquie, en Iran et en Arabie Saoudite.

Reporters sans Frontières a besoin d'argent pour défendre les journalistes en prison et pour aider les familles de ceux qui sont morts ou qui ont dû fuir leur pays. Donc trois journalistes très connus en France ont décidé de vendre, dans les magasins de journaux, une collection de leurs photographies: "Pour la liberté de la presse". C'est une campagne "choc" pour la défense de la liberté de la presse.

(*a*) Journalists are often banned from writing about certain things in countries like China, Turkey, etc. Why is this?

1

_____

(*b*) The organisation "Reporters sans Frontières" is always trying to raise money. Why? Mention **three** things.

3

_____

_____

_____

(*c*) Three well known French journalists have agreed to help. What have they decided to do?

1

_____

[Turn over

Marks

4. You come across this article about Robbie Williams.

Robbie Williams . . . une drôle de vie!

Robert Peter Williams est né le 13 février 1974 à Newcastle. Ses parents ont divorcé quand Robbie avait trois ans et après, il a vécu avec sa mère, Theresa. Il a aussi une soeur aînée, Sally.

C'est un neveu de sa soeur qui a trouvé pour Robbie son premier emploi: vendeur de fenêtres à double vitrage.

Les premières années de sa vie, il habitait une maison tout près d'un stade où s'entraînait Port Vale FC, son équipe préférée. A l'école, il était plutôt bon élève; il avait toujours de bonnes notes dans la plupart des matières.

Comme son père, Robbie se destinait à la comédie, mais à l'âge de 16 ans, il a été engagé pour former le groupe Take That. Après avoir quitté le groupe très fâché contre le producteur, il s'est lancé dans une carrière solo qui a mis plusieurs années à démarrer. Voilà pourquoi il a sombré dans l'alcool et la drogue.

Libéré de ses démons, Robbie a signé avec sa maison de disques un énorme contrat qui l'abritera du besoin d'argent jusqu' à la fin de ses jours.

(*a*) What was Robbie's first job and how did he get it?

2

_____

_____

(*b*) How did he become a fan of Port Vale FC?

1

_____

(*c*) What are we told about his schooldays? Mention **one** thing.

1

_____

(*d*) According to the article, why did he have problems with alcohol and drugs?

1

_____

(*e*) What will be the outcome of his new recording contract?

1

_____

Page six

Marks

5. The article on Robbie Williams continues with an interview.

Robbie: "J'adore venir en France . . ."

... interviewé par Claire Richard.

C.R. Tu as acheté une maison à Los Angeles et tu passes pas mal de temps en Californie. Alors, tu déménages aux Etats-Unis?

R.W. Non, je passe du temps dans le monde entier. Je voyage de pays en pays pour faire des concerts.

C.R. Tu vas bientôt donner deux concerts à Paris. Comment seront-ils, ces concerts?

R.W. Je ne sais pas exactement encore, mais il y aura des feux d'artifice. Ce seront, sans doute, des spectacles inoubliables!

C.R. Oui, tu commences à être bien apprécié en France. Il ne reste pas de billets pour les concerts.

R.W. C'est vrai, mais je ne sais pas si les Français me connaissent si bien que ça. Quand je fais des concerts en France ce sont les Britanniques qui achètent la plupart des billets. Quand même, j'adore venir en France. Les gens sont très sympas.

C.R. Et le côté romantique?

R.W. Dans le passé, j'ai eu beaucoup de petites copines et j'en aurai encore. Je trouve difficile de résister à une belle fille.

(*a*) Why does the interviewer think Robbie is moving to the USA?
Mention any **one** thing.   1

_____

(*b*) What will his concerts in Paris be like? Mention **one** thing.   1

_____

(*c*) According to Robbie, why are his French concerts so well-attended?   1

_____

(*d*) What does Robbie say about girls? Mention any **two** things.   2

_____

_____

[BLANK PAGE]

C

1000/409

NATIONAL QUALIFICATIONS 2005	TUESDAY, 10 MAY 2.30 PM – 3.00 PM (APPROX)	FRENCH STANDARD GRADE Credit Level Listening Transcript

This paper must not be seen by any candidate.

The material overleaf is provided for use in an emergency only (eg the recording or equipment proving faulty) or where permission has been given in advance by SQA for the material to be read to candidates with special needs. The material must be read exactly as printed.

SCOTTISH
QUALIFICATIONS
AUTHORITY

Transcript—Credit Level

> **Instructions to reader(s):**
>
> For each item, read the English **once,** then read the French **three times**, with an interval of 5 seconds between the readings. On completion of the third reading, pause for the length of time indicated in brackets after each item, to allow the candidates to write their answers.
>
> Where special arrangements have been agreed in advance to allow the reading of the material, those sections marked **(f)** should be read by a female speaker and those marked **(m)** by a male: those sections marked **(t)** should be read by the teacher.

(t) You are taking part in an exchange visit to France. When you arrive at your pen friend Marc's house, you learn that he is in hospital and you go to visit him.

(m)
or
(f)
Tu participes à un échange scolaire en France. Quand tu arrives chez ton correspondant Marc, tu apprends qu'il est à l'hôpital et tu vas le voir.

(t) Question number one.

Marc tells you about the events leading up to him being in hospital. What does he say? Mention **two** things.

(m) **Samedi dernier c'était la Fête de la Musique dans le village. L'après-midi il y avait au moins douze orchestres et beaucoup de danseurs dans la rue principale.**

(40 seconds)

(t) Question number two.

He goes on to explain what happened to him. What does he say? Mention any **two** things.

(m) **Dans la rue il y avait énormément de spectateurs. On m'a poussé par derrière et je suis tombé. J'ai su immédiatement que c'était grave. Et, ici, à l'hôpital, ils ont diagnostiqué une jambe cassée.**

(40 seconds)

(t) Question number three.

He tells you about his stay in hospital. Why was he not happy at first? Why is he happier now?

(m) **Au début, j'étais dans une salle avec beaucoup de personnes âgées, mais maintenant ça va mieux parce que je suis dans une chambre avec trois personnes de mon âge.**

(40 seconds)

(t) Question number four.

He tells you about the food in the hospital. What does he say? Mention any **two** things.

(m) **Les repas ne sont pas aussi bons que chez moi. Parfois il y a des plats que je n'aime pas du tout. Alors, je téléphone à ma mère et elle m'apporte quelque chose à manger.**

(40 seconds)

(t) Question number five.

When will Marc get home from hospital? What does he suggest you do till then?

(m)   Je dois rester à l'hôpital jusqu'à la fin de la semaine. Donc, je propose que tu passes ces quatre jours chez mon ami, Gérard, qui habite pas loin d'ici.

(40 seconds)

(t) Question number six.

When you arrive at Gérard's house, his mother speaks to you. How long have Marc and Gérard known each other? How did they get to know each other? Mention any **two** things.

(f)   Marc et Gérard se connaissent depuis onze ans. A ce moment-là, nos deux familles habitaient la même rue. Les deux garçons avaient le même âge, donc ils étaient dans la même classe à l'école primaire.

(40 seconds)

(t) Question number seven.

You are introduced to Gérard, who tells you what he and Marc used to do every day. What did they do? Mention any **two** things. What happened in the evenings?

(m)   On se voyait tous les jours. Le matin, on allait à l'école à vélo; à midi, on mangeait à la cantine, et on rentrait ensemble à la fin de la journée. Après le repas du soir, ou bien Marc venait chez moi, ou bien j'allais chez lui pour jouer.

(40 seconds)

(t) Question number eight.

What did the boys do on holiday last year? Mention any **two** things. What was Gérard particularly pleased about?

(m)   L'année dernière, nous sommes partis en vacances ensemble. Nous avons passé un mois à la montagne. On a fait beaucoup d'activités—des randonnées à cheval, de l'escalade et du ski nautique. Ce qui m'a vraiment plu, c'est qu'on a fait la connaissance de beaucoup de jeunes de tous les coins de la France.

(40 seconds)

(t) Question number nine.

Gérard goes on to talk about the future. Complete the sentences.

(m)   Marc et moi, nous allons peut-être nous retrouver à l'université. Comme tu le sais déjà, Marc est fort en langues vivantes; et moi, je voudrais devenir pharmacien. De toute façon, je suis sûr que j'ai trouvé un ami pour toute la vie.

(40 seconds)

[Turn over for Question 10 on *Page four*

(t) Question number ten.

According to Gérard's mother, how will life at home change when Gérard goes to university? Mention any **one** thing. What do Gérard's parents complain about at the moment? Mention any **two** things.

(f)   Quand Gérard partira pour l'université, la vie chez nous sera beaucoup plus tranquille. En ce moment, il y a souvent des disputes à la maison. Son père et moi, on trouve que Gérard rentre trop tard à la maison pendant la semaine; il laisse toujours sa chambre en désordre, et puis, il passe trop de temps devant la télévision.

(40 seconds)

(t) End of test.

Now look over your answers.

[END OF TRANSCRIPT]

Total
Marks

1000/408

NATIONAL
QUALIFICATIONS
2005

TUESDAY, 10 MAY
2.30 PM – 3.00 PM
(APPROX)

**FRENCH
STANDARD GRADE**
Credit Level
Listening

Fill in these boxes and read what is printed below.

Full name of centre

Town

Forename(s)

Surname

Date of birth

Day Month Year

Scottish candidate number

Number of seat

When you are told to do so, open your paper.

You will hear a number of short items in French. You will hear each item three times, then you will have time to write your answer.

Write your answers, **in English**, in this book, in the appropriate spaces.

You may take notes as you are listening to the French, but only in this paper.

You may **not** use a French dictionary.

You are not allowed to leave the examination room until the end of the test.

Before leaving the examination room you must give this book to the invigilator. If you do not, you may lose all the marks for this paper.

SCOTTISH
QUALIFICATIONS
AUTHORITY

Marks

You are taking part in an exchange visit to France. When you arrive at your pen friend Marc's house, you learn that he is in hospital and you go to visit him.

Tu participes à un échange scolaire en France. Quand tu arrives chez ton correspondant Marc, tu apprends qu'il est à l'hôpital et tu vas le voir.

1. Marc tells you about the events leading up to him being in hospital. What does he say? Mention **two** things.

_____

_____

2

*   *   *   *   *

2. He goes on to explain what happened to him. What does he say? Mention any **two** things.

_____

_____

2

*   *   *   *   *

3. He tells you about his stay in hospital.

    (a) Why was he not happy at first?

    _____

1

    (b) Why is he happier now?

    _____

1

*   *   *   *   *

4. He tells you about the food in the hospital. What does he say? Mention any **two** things.

_____

_____

2

*   *   *   *   *

Marks

5. (*a*) When will Marc get home from hospital?   1

_____

(*b*) What does he suggest you do till then?   1

_____

_____

*   *   *   *   *

6. When you arrive at Gérard's house, his mother speaks to you.

(*a*) How long have Marc and Gérard known each other?   1

_____

(*b*) How did they get to know each other? Mention any **two** things.   2

_____

_____

*   *   *   *   *

7. You are introduced to Gérard, who tells you what he and Marc used to do every day.

(*a*) What did they do? Mention any **two** things.   2

_____

_____

(*b*) What happened in the evenings?   1

_____

*   *   *   *   *

[Turn over for Questions 8 to 10 on *Page four*

Marks

8. (*a*) What did the boys do on holiday last year? Mention any **two** things.   2

_____

_____

(*b*) What was Gérard particularly pleased about?   1

_____

*   *   *   *   *

9. Gérard goes on to talk about the future. Complete the sentences.   3

Both boys hope to go to university.

Marc is good at _____.

Gérard wants to be _____.

Gérard is sure that he has found _____.

*   *   *   *   *

10. (*a*) According to Gérard's mother, how will life at home change when Gérard goes to university? Mention any **one** thing.   1

_____

(*b*) What do Gérard's parents complain about at the moment? Mention any **two** things.   2

_____

_____

*   *   *   *   *

Total (25)

[*END OF QUESTION PAPER*]

2006 | Credit

[BLANK PAGE]

FOR OFFICIAL USE

C

Total

1000/403

NATIONAL
QUALIFICATIONS
2006

TUESDAY, 9 MAY
11.10 AM – 12.10 PM

FRENCH
STANDARD GRADE
Credit Level
Reading

Fill in these boxes and read what is printed below.

Full name of centre

Town

Forename(s)

Surname

Date of birth
Day Month Year

Scottish candidate number

Number of seat

When you are told to do so, open your paper and write your answers **in English** in the spaces provided.

You may use a French dictionary.

Before leaving the examination room you must give this book to the invigilator. If you do not, you may lose all the marks for this paper.

SCOTTISH
QUALIFICATIONS
AUTHORITY

PB 1000/403 6/23970

Marks

You are reading a French magazine.

1. A girl has written to the advice page of the magazine with some concerns about smoking.

Chère Anne!

Beaucoup de mes amies fument déjà, et elles n'arrêtent pas de me dire que fumer c'est extra, et que je devrais essayer.

J'ai peur qu'elles ne me parlent plus si je refuse de fumer avec elles. Que dois-je faire?

Bernadette, 13 ans.

Complete the sentences.

(a) Bernadette's friends say that smoking is _____   **2**

and that she _____ .

(b) If Bernadette refuses, she is afraid that her friends _____   **1**

_____ .

Marks

2. The editor of the magazine has answered Bernadette's letter.

> Fumer ou ne pas fumer, c'est une décision pour chaque individu.
>
> Il faut savoir que . . .
>
> . . . presque la moitié des jeunes Français âgés de 15 à 24 ans fument.
>
> . . . les filles qui fument sont de plus en plus nombreuses et elles sont plus jeunes quand elles commencent à fumer.
>
> Dans quelques années, tes copines auront la mauvaise haleine et les doigts jaunes – sans parler de maladies bien plus graves. En expliquant tout ça à tes copines, tu peux leur montrer que tu as de très bonnes raisons pour dire "non" à la cigarette.
>
> Tu sais que, depuis le début de l'année, les médias refusent de donner une image positive des fumeurs. Au contraire ils informent le public des dangers du tabac pour la santé.

(a) What statistic is given about French people between the ages of 15 and 24?　　**1**

_____

(b) What information is given about girls? Mention any **one** thing.　　**1**

_____

_____

(c) What problems will Bernadette's friends have in a few years? Mention any **two** things.　　**2**

_____

_____

(d) How are the media helping in the campaign against smoking? Mention any **one** thing.　　**1**

_____

[Turn over

Marks

3. You come across an article about an environmental problem.

La France sous les déchets

Vous avez vu tous les emballages qu'on jette à la poubelle quand on revient du supermarché? La société est devenue trop gourmande en emballage. En 1975 un Français produisait 500g d'ordures ménagères par jour. Aujourd'hui il en produit un kilo.

Le Ministre de l'Ecologie lance un plan d'action. Elle demande aux consommateurs de faire des efforts pour utiliser moins d'emballages. Comme ça on va gaspiller moins de papier.

Une grande campagne de publicité va encourager les Français à acheter des produits qui respectent l'environnement et à réutiliser les sacs plastiques.

(*a*) What has doubled since 1975?

1

_____

_____

(*b*) (i) What does the Minister for the Environment want people to do?

2

_____

(ii) Why?

_____

(*c*) What is the purpose of the publicity campaign? Mention **two** things.

2

_____

_____

Marks

4. You read an article about the work of a pharmacist.

> ### Marcel, 52 ans, pharmacien dans un village du Haut-Rhin.
>
> Je voulais faire quelque chose dans le domaine des sciences et au lycée j'aimais la biochimie et la physique, donc j'ai étudié la pharmacologie à l'université.
>
> Les pharmaciens ont six ans d'étude après le bac, donc ils finissent leurs études assez tard, à l'âge de 23 ans ou plus. Deux pharmaciens sur trois travaillent dans les pharmacies et les autres dans les laboratoires des hôpitaux et chez les fabricants de médicaments.
>
> Pour faire ce métier, il faut s'intéresser aux gens et s'entendre bien avec ses clients. Mes clients me racontent leurs problèmes de santé et je leur explique les ordonnances.

(a) Why did Marcel choose to study pharmacy? Mention any **one** thing.　　1

_____

_____

(b) What does he say about becoming a pharmacist? Mention any **one** thing.　1

_____

_____

(c) Apart from pharmacies, where do most pharmacists work? Mention **two** things.　　2

_____

_____

(d) What does he say about his job? Mention any **two** things.　　2

_____

_____

[Turn over

Marks

5. You read an article in which young French people discuss whether machines are good or bad for society.

Les machines nous apportent des biens. Oui! Mais ......

Chantal: Prenons le téléphone, par exemple. Cela nous permet de parler à une personne qui se trouve à des dizaines, même des centaines, de kilomètres. C'est quelque chose qui facilitie la vie, mais par conséquence, il y a moins de courrier et donc, moins de travail, et peut-être le chômage pour les facteurs.

Mathieu: Plus on a de machines, plus on a de besoins. Par exemple, on a inventé le portable. Mais, pour les faire fonctionner, on a besoin de chargeurs et d'un réseau.

Thierry: Et maintenant il y a les ordinateurs. Dans l'avenir, les ordinateurs feront tout le travail des hommes, mais les gens ne vont pas s'ennuyer. Au lieu de travailler, ils pourront consacrer tout leur temps à s'amuser.

(*a*) According to Chantal the telephone has been a useful invention. But, what are the disadvantages? Mention any **two** things.　　2

_____

_____

(*b*) What invention does Mathieu talk about?　　1

_____

(*c*) Why is it of little use on its own?　　1

_____

(*d*) What does Thierry say about the effect of computers? Mention **three** things.　　3

_____

_____

[END OF QUESTION PAPER]　　**Total (26)**

C

1000/409

NATIONAL
QUALIFICATIONS
2006

TUESDAY, 9 MAY
2.30 PM – 3.00 PM
(APPROX)

FRENCH
STANDARD GRADE
Credit Level
Listening Transcript

This paper must not be seen by any candidate.

The material overleaf is provided for use in an emergency only (eg the recording or equipment proving faulty) or where permission has been given in advance by SQA for the material to be read to candidates with additional support needs. The material must be read exactly as printed.

SCOTTISH
QUALIFICATIONS
AUTHORITY

©

Transcript—Credit Level

Instructions to reader(s):

For each item, read the English **once,** then read the French **three times,** with an interval of 5 seconds between the readings. On completion of the third reading, pause for the length of time indicated in brackets after each item, to allow the candidates to write their answers.

Where special arrangements have been agreed in advance to allow the reading of the material, those sections marked **(f)** should be read by a female speaker and those marked **(m)** by a male: those sections marked **(t)** should be read by the teacher.

(t) You are spending your holidays with your family in a hotel in France.

(m) or (f) **Tu passes les vacances avec ta famille dans un hôtel en France.**

(t) Question number one.

You meet a French boy called Georges who introduces you to his twin sister, Nicole. What does he say?

(m) **Voici ma soeur, Nicole. Nous sommes jumeaux. Heureusement, nous nous entendons très bien. J'ai de très bons rapports avec elle.**

(40 seconds)

(t) Question number two.

Georges' mother tells you about their holidays. What does she say? Mention any **two** things.

(f) **En général, on passe seulement une semaine ici en juillet parce que mon mari doit travailler. Pour nous, les vacances principales sont en hiver. Nous passons une quinzaine à faire du ski en Suisse.**

(40 seconds)

(t) Question number three.

She then explains what there is to do in the area. What does she say? Mention any **two** things.

(f) **Passer les vacances ici, ça me plaît beaucoup. Il y a tant de choses à faire pour les jeunes. Il y a un parc d'attractions pas loin d'ici. Et en plus, on peut faire de l'équitation.**

(40 seconds)

(t) Question number four.

Georges talks about his sporting activities. What does he tell you? Mention any **two** things.

(m) **Moi, j'ai la chance d'être doué pour le sport. Je fais des sports d'équipe et des sports individuels. Au collège, je suis champion de natation.**

(40 seconds)

(t) Question number five.

What did he do during the Easter holidays? Mention any **two** things.

(m) Pendant les vacances de Pâques, j'ai travaillé dans un club pour les enfants âgés de cinq à dix ans. C'était une expérience formidable pour moi! J'ai passé toute la journée en plein air avec les enfants.

(40 seconds)

(t) Question number six.

What does Georges say about his school subjects? What does he say about the kind of job he wants? Mention any **one** thing.

(m) Je ne suis pas fort en maths et en français. Être assis dans un bureau ne m'intéresse pas du tout. Je sais que je dois trouver un métier où je serai tout le temps actif.

(40 seconds)

(t) Question number seven.

Nicole tells you she wants to be a librarian. What does she say about her childhood which shows her interest in books? Mention **two** things.

(f) Depuis très longtemps, je veux devenir bibliothécaire. Quand j'étais enfant, je lisais avec enthousiasme des livres de toutes sortes. Quelquefois, j'oubliais de venir manger avec la famille parce que je voulais finir mon livre.

(40 seconds)

(t) Question number eight.

What has Nicole done to prepare herself for the job of librarian? Mention **two** things.

(f) Au mois de juillet, j'ai travaillé dans la bibliothèque municipale de notre ville. J'ai remplacé un bibliothécaire qui était en vacances. C'était intéressant et très utile pour moi.

(40 seconds)

(t) Question number nine.

Libraries are not just for lending books. For what other reasons do people go there? Mention **two** things.

(f) Tu sais, aujourd'hui, le travail de bibliothécaire ne consiste pas seulement à distribuer les livres. Dans presque toutes les bibliothèques, on trouve des ordinateurs et beaucoup de gens viennent chercher des informations sur Internet. Et il y a aussi des étudiants qui doivent faire des recherches pour préparer leurs examens.

(40 seconds)

[Turn over for Questions 10 to 13 on *Page four*

(t) **Question number ten.**

Their father talks about his first job helping his uncle. What did his uncle do for a living? How did he help him?

(m) **Mon oncle avait une petite ferme où il cultivait des fruits et des légumes. A l'âge de quinze ans, je l'aidais à transporter les produits au marché tous les samedi matins.**

(*40 seconds*)

(t) **Question number eleven.**

What does Nicole say about her mother? She sometimes has problems with her dad. Why? Mention any **one** thing.

(f) **Dans l'ensemble, ma mère me traite comme une adulte mais quelquefois j'ai des problèmes avec mon père. Il est protecteur quand je veux sortir. Il ne comprend pas que je ne suis plus une enfant.**

(*40 seconds*)

(t) **Question number twelve.**

Their mother also talks about what happens when young people go to university. What does she say? Mention any **two** things.

(f) **Quand les jeunes vont à l'université ils veulent être indépendants, bien sûr! Mais ils sont souvent influencés par les autres et il y a toujours la tentation de prendre de la drogue ou de trop boire.**

(*40 seconds*)

(t) **Question number thirteen.**

What does their father say about Nicole and Georges and the work they will do? Mention any **two** things.

(m) **Nicole et Georges, ils sont très différents l'un de l'autre. Mais ce qu'ils feront dans la vie ne m'inquiète pas. L'important, c'est qu'ils trouvent un métier où ils sont heureux, un emploi qui leur plaît.**

(*40 seconds*)

(t) **End of test.**

Now look over your answers.

[END OF TRANSCRIPT]

FOR OFFICIAL USE

C

Total Marks

1000/408

NATIONAL
QUALIFICATIONS
2006

TUESDAY, 9 MAY
2.30 PM – 3.00 PM
(APPROX)

**FRENCH
STANDARD GRADE**
Credit Level
Listening

Fill in these boxes and read what is printed below.

Full name of centre

Town

Forename(s)

Surname

Date of birth

Day Month Year   Scottish candidate number   Number of seat

When you are told to do so, open your paper.

You will hear a number of short items in French. You will hear each item three times, then you will have time to write your answer.

Write your answers, **in English**, in this book, in the appropriate spaces.

You may take notes as you are listening to the French, but only in this paper.

You may **not** use a French dictionary.

You are not allowed to leave the examination room until the end of the test.

Before leaving the examination room you must give this book to the invigilator. If you do not, you may lose all the marks for this paper.

SCOTTISH
QUALIFICATIONS
AUTHORITY

PB 1000/408 6/23970

Marks

You are spending your holidays with your family in a hotel in France.

Tu passes les vacances avec ta famille dans un hôtel en France.

1. You meet a French boy called Georges who introduces you to his twin sister, Nicole. What does he say?

_____

_____

1

*   *   *   *   *

2. Georges' mother tells you about their holidays. What does she say? Mention any **two** things.

_____

_____

2

*   *   *   *   *

3. She then explains what there is to do in the area. What does she say? Mention any **two** things.

_____

_____

2

*   *   *   *   *

4. Georges talks about his sporting activities. What does he tell you? Mention any **two** things.

_____

_____

2

*   *   *   *   *

Page two

Marks

5. What did he do during the Easter holidays? Mention any **two** things.

_____

_____

2

*　　*　　*　　*　　*

6. (*a*)　What does Georges say about his school subjects?

_____

_____

1

(*b*)　What does he say about the kind of job he wants? Mention any **one** thing.

_____

_____

1

*　　*　　*　　*　　*

7. Nicole tells you she wants to be a librarian. What does she say about her childhood which shows her interest in books? Mention **two** things.

_____

_____

2

*　　*　　*　　*　　*

8. What has Nicole done to prepare herself for the job of librarian? Mention **two** things.

_____

_____

2

*　　*　　*　　*　　*

[Turn over

Marks

9. Libraries are not just for lending books. For what other reasons do people go there? Mention **two** things.

2

_____

_____

*   *   *   *   *

10. Their father talks about his first job helping his uncle.

    (*a*) What did his uncle do for a living?

1

    _____

    (*b*) How did he help him?

1

    _____

*   *   *   *   *

11. (*a*) What does Nicole say about her mother?

1

    _____

    (*b*) She sometimes has problems with her dad. Why? Mention any **one** thing.

1

    _____

*   *   *   *   *

12. Their mother also talks about what happens when young people go to university. What does she say? Mention any **two** things.

2

_____

_____

*   *   *   *   *

Marks

13. What does their father say about Nicole and Georges and the work they will do? Mention any **two** things.

2

_____

_____

* * * * *

Total (25)

[*END OF QUESTION PAPER*]

[BLANK PAGE]

[BLANK PAGE]

C

FOR OFFICIAL USE

Total

1000/403

NATIONAL
QUALIFICATIONS
2007

WEDNESDAY, 9 MAY
11.10 AM – 12.10 PM

FRENCH
STANDARD GRADE
Credit Level
Reading

Fill in these boxes and read what is printed below.

Full name of centre

Town

Forename(s)

Surname

Date of birth
Day   Month   Year

Scottish candidate number

Number of seat

When you are told to do so, open your paper and write your answers **in English** in the spaces provided.

You may use a French dictionary.

Before leaving the examination room you must give this book to the invigilator. If you do not, you may lose all the marks for this paper.

SCOTTISH
QUALIFICATIONS
AUTHORITY

©

Marks

1. Some young French people have written to a website with their views on being an only child.

Être enfant unique—avantage ou inconvénient?

Moi, je suis fille unique et ce n'est pas du tout un inconvénient. Mais, on a des problèmes familiaux quand même.

Je crois que je reçois plus d'attention de mes parents parce que je suis seule, mais mes parents me mettent aussi beaucoup de pression avec mes études.

On ne devrait pas comparer la vie seule à la vie avec des frères et des soeurs parce qu'on ne peut rien changer.

Marion (Rouen)

Je suis enfant unique et cela me va très bien. Je ne peux pas m'imaginer avec un frère ou une soeur. Je ne me sens pas seul, parce que je ne manque pas d'amis au collège.

Si j'avais un frère, il faudrait tout partager—les bonbons, les cadeaux, l'argent de poche, peut-être ma chambre. Quelle horreur!

Thierry (Boulogne)

(*a*) According to Marion, what is the advantage of being an only child? **1**

_____

(*b*) What disadvantage is there for her? **1**

_____

(*c*) Why does she think you should not compare being an only child with having brothers and sisters? **1**

_____

(*d*) Thierry does not feel lonely. Why? **1**

_____

(*e*) Why would he not like to have a brother? **1**

_____

Page two

Marks

2. This article gives advice to parents who are worried about children who have an untidy room.

Quel bazar* dans la chambre!

Pour éduquer un enfant à garder de l'ordre dans sa chambre, il faut commencer tôt.

A partir de trois ans, on peut demander à l'enfant de mettre son nounours sur une chaise et de ramasser ses jouets. Ne dites jamais: "Range ta chambre", parce que c'est une idée que l'enfant est incapable de comprendre. Pour un enfant de sept à huit ans on peut dire: "Ne laisse pas traîner tes affaires par terre" et "Rapporte les verres et les assiettes sales à la cuisine".

***bazar** = a mess

2

(a) To teach a child to keep his room in order, what must a parent do?

1

_____

(b) What can a three-year old be asked to do? Mention **two** things.

2

_____

3

_____

(c) What should parents never say to a three-year old?

1

_____

(d) What reason is given for this?

1

_____

(e) What can a parent ask a seven or eight-year old child to do? Mention **two** things.

2

_____

_____

[Turn over

Marks

3. The article about bringing up children continues.

> A partir de douze ans, l'enfant considère sa chambre comme son espace personnel. Donc, les parents doivent prendre l'habitude de frapper avant d'entrer.
>
> Pour les adolescents, il faut leur faire comprendre que la chambre fait partie de la maison. Donc, ils n'ont pas le droit de peindre les murs sans la permission de parents.
>
> En ce qui concerne la musique, on ne doit pas accepter qu'ils jouent du "Rap" très fort sur le mp3, puisqu'il y a un risque de surdité.
>
> On peut insister aussi sur la propreté. Les ados doivent passer l'aspirateur dans la chambre tous les quinze jours et ils doivent mettre leurs vêtements sales dans le panier à linge une fois par semaine.

(a) What should parents do when children reach the age of twelve?   **1**

_____

(b) If teenagers want to do something to their room what do they have to understand? Mention any **one** thing.   **1**

_____

(c) Why are parents entitled to insist that the volume of the mp3 player be kept down?   **1**

_____

(d) What should parents insist that young people do to keep their room tidy? Mention **two** things.   **2**

_____

_____

4. You then read an article about people who move to other countries.

POURQUOI QUITTER SON PAYS?

Un habitant du monde sur trente-cinq est immigré: une personne qui quitte son pays pour aller vivre dans un pays plus développé, pour trouver du travail et de meilleures conditions de vie. Mais beaucoup des pays qui les accueillent ne sont pas nécessairement riches. Souvent les entreprises et les usines sont en train de se développer et elles ont besoin d'employés.

Dans les pays d'accueil, ces immigrations peuvent poser des difficultés. Les immigrés s'installent parfois dans les régions où il y a moins de possibilités de travail et où il y a déjà beaucoup de chômage.

(*a*) Why does one person in 35 in the world leave his/her own country? Mention any **two** things.

2

_____

_____

(*b*) What information are we given about the countries people move to? Mention any **two** things.

2

_____

_____

(*c*) What difficulties can sometimes arise? Mention **two** things.

2

_____

_____

[Turn over

DO NO'
WRITE
THIS
MARGI

Marks

5. The article continues.

> Peut-être que ces immigrations pourraient être plus bénéfiques si elles étaient mieux organisées: par exemple, si on encourageait les immigrés à chercher des pays qui sont capables de leur offrir du travail. En ce moment, dans certains pays où ils vont, leur rêve de trouver du travail est souvent déçu. Par conséquent, ils n'ont pas de domicile fixe, pas de papiers et ils se retrouvent dans la pauvreté.

(a) It is suggested that immigration could be better organised. In what way?   **1**

_____

_____

(b) What are the consequences for people who do not find work? Mention any **two** things.   **2**

_____

_____

Total (26)

[END OF QUESTION PAPER]

C

1000/409

NATIONAL
QUALIFICATIONS
2007

WEDNESDAY, 9 MAY
2.30 PM – 3.00 PM
(APPROX)

FRENCH
STANDARD GRADE
Credit Level
Listening Transcript

This paper must not be seen by any candidate.

The material overleaf is provided for use in an emergency only (eg the recording or equipment proving faulty) or where permission has been given in advance by SQA for the material to be read to candidates with additional support needs. The material must be read exactly as printed.

SCOTTISH
QUALIFICATIONS
AUTHORITY

©

Transcript—Credit Level

> **Instructions to reader(s):**
>
> For each item, read the English **once,** then read the French **three times**, with an interval of 5 seconds between the readings. On completion of the third reading, pause for the length of time indicated in brackets after each item, to allow the candidates to write their answers.
>
> Where special arrangements have been agreed in advance to allow the reading of the material, those sections marked **(f)** should be read by a female speaker and those marked **(m)** by a male: those sections marked **(t)** should be read by the teacher.

(t) You are spending a holiday with Francine, your French pen-pal.

(m) or (f) **Tu passes des vacances chez Francine, ta correspondante française.**

(t) Question number one.

Francine says you will be going to a club tonight. What does she say about the club? Complete the sentences.

(f) **Ce soir, on va en boîte avec les copains. Le vendredi soir, c'est très populaire et il y a toujours beaucoup de monde. Mais si on arrive avant neuf heures, c'est gratuit pour les filles. Elles ne paient pas.**

(40 seconds)

(t) Question number two.

Francine talks about going out at night. What does she say? Complete the sentence.

(f) **Je trouve que mes parents sont compréhensifs. Ils me permettent de sortir très tard si je leur dis où je vais, et avec qui.**

(40 seconds)

(t) Question number three.

Why is she not afraid when she is out late in town? Mention **two** things.

(f) **Je n'ai pas peur quand je suis en ville après minuit, car je ne suis jamais seule; j'ai toujours mes copines avec moi. Et puis, j'ai mon portable dans ma poche.**

(40 seconds)

(t) Question number four.

Francine talks about her parents. What does she say about her mother? Mention any **one** thing. What sometimes causes arguments with her father?

(f) **Je m'entends bien avec ma mère; je trouve qu'elle a des opinions et des attitudes très jeunes, très modernes. En général, ça va avec mon père aussi. Mais parfois, il y a des disputes qui sont provoquées par des questions d'argent.**

(40 seconds)

(t) Question number five.

What does Francine think about the pocket money she receives? What is her father's opinion?

(f)   **Mes parents me donnent de l'argent de poche, mais cela ne me suffit pas. J'aimerais avoir un peu plus d'argent, mais mon père dit que je devrais trouver un travail le week-end.**

(40 seconds)

(t) Question number six.

Where does Francine hope to go in the summer? What will she find difficult?

(f)   **En juillet, mes copines et moi, nous voulons partir dans un village de vacances à la montagne. C'est uniquement pour les adolescents. Bien sûr, je devrai faire des économies, et ça, c'est très difficile pour moi.**

(40 seconds)

(t) Question number seven.

What activities will be available during the day? Mention any **one** thing. What will they do in the evenings?

n) or (f)   **Pendant la journée, on pourra faire de l'escalade et des randonnées à cheval. Et, le soir, on va discuter des projets du lendemain.**

(40 seconds)

(t) Question number eight.

Why is Francine looking forward to the holiday so much?

(f)   **Ce sera formidable parce que je vais passer un mois entier avec des jeunes de mon âge!**

(40 seconds)

(t) One evening you are listening to a French radio station. You hear an interview with Jacques Lambert, a French footballer who plays for a Scottish team.

(t) Question number nine.

What does Jacques say about his links with Scotland? Mention any **two** things.

(m)   **Ça fait trois ans que j'habite en Ecosse et je viens d'acheter une nouvelle maison sur la côte ouest. Ma femme et moi, nous avons de très bons amis là-bas.**

(40 seconds)

[Turn over for Questions 10 to 13 on *Page four*

(t) Question number ten.

What difficulties did he have when he first arrived? Mention **two** things.

(m)   **Au début, je ne connaissais personne. Et, en plus, j'avais du mal à comprendre les Ecossais à cause de leur accent.**

(40 seconds)

(t) Question number eleven.

What does Jacques say about the players in his team? Mention any **one** thing. What do the coaches have to do?

(m)   **Dans notre équipe il y a des joueurs qui viennent de différents pays, et ils parlent plusieurs langues. Donc, quand les entraîneurs nous parlent en anglais, ils sont obligés de parler lentement.**

(40 seconds)

(t) Question number twelve.

What does he not like about living in Scotland? What problem does this cause?

(m)   **Je dois admettre que le climat m'énerve énormément. On ne sait jamais s'il va faire beau, donc on ne peut pas organiser facilement des activités en plein air.**

(40 seconds)

(t) Question number thirteen.

What was Jacques' childhood like? Mention any **one** thing. What is his life like now? Mention any **one** thing.

(m)   **Quand j'étais jeune, ma famille était assez pauvre. On habitait dans un tout petit appartement et on n'avait pas de voiture. Maintenant, je n'ai pas de problèmes financiers et j'ai la possibilité de voir le monde.**

(40 seconds)

(t) End of test.

Now look over your answers.

[END OF TRANSCRIPT]

FOR OFFICIAL USE

C

Total Marks

1000/408

NATIONAL
QUALIFICATIONS
2007

WEDNESDAY, 9 MAY
2.30 PM – 3.00 PM
(APPROX)

**FRENCH
STANDARD GRADE**
Credit Level
Listening

Fill in these boxes and read what is printed below.

Full name of centre

Town

Forename(s)

Surname

Date of birth

Day Month Year   Scottish candidate number   Number of seat

When you are told to do so, open your paper.

You will hear a number of short items in French. You will hear each item three times, then you will have time to write your answer.

Write your answers, **in English**, in this book, in the appropriate spaces.

You may take notes as you are listening to the French, but only in this paper.

You may **not** use a French dictionary.

You are not allowed to leave the examination room until the end of the test.

Before leaving the examination room you must give this book to the invigilator. If you do not, you may lose all the marks for this paper.

SCOTTISH
QUALIFICATIONS
AUTHORITY

Marks

You are spending a holiday with Francine, your French pen-pal.

Tu passes des vacances chez Francine, ta correspondante française.

1. Francine says you will be going to a club tonight. What does she say about the club? Complete the sentences.   **2**

   On Fridays, the club _____

   _____ .

   Before nine o'clock _____ .

   *   *   *   *   *

2. Francine talks about going out at night. What does she say? Complete the sentence.   **2**

   Her parents let her go out late if _____

   _____ and _____ .

   *   *   *   *   *

3. Why is she not afraid when she is out late in town? Mention **two** things.   **2**

   _____

   _____

   *   *   *   *   *

4. Francine talks about her parents.

   (*a*) What does she say about her mother? Mention any **one** thing.   **1**

   _____

   (*b*) What sometimes causes arguments with her father?   **1**

   _____

   *   *   *   *   *

Marks

5. (*a*)   What does Francine think about the pocket money she receives?

_____   **1**

(*b*)   What is her father's opinion?

_____   **1**

*   *   *   *   *

6. (*a*)   Where does Francine hope to go in the summer?

_____   **1**

(*b*)   What will she find difficult?

_____   **1**

*   *   *   *   *

7. (*a*)   What activities will be available during the day?   Mention any **one** thing.

_____

_____   **1**

(*b*)   What will they do in the evenings?

_____   **1**

*   *   *   *   *

8.   Why is Francine looking forward to the holiday so much?

_____   **1**

*   *   *   *   *

[Turn over

Marks

One evening you are listening to a French radio station. You hear an interview with Jacques Lambert, a French footballer who plays for a Scottish team.

9. What does Jacques say about his links with Scotland? Mention any **two** things.

2

_____

_____

* * * * *

10. What difficulties did he have when he first arrived? Mention **two** things.

2

_____

_____

* * * * *

11. (*a*) What does Jacques say about the players in his team? Mention any **one** thing.

1

_____

(*b*) What do the coaches have to do?

1

_____

* * * * *

12. (*a*) What does he not like about living in Scotland?

1

_____

(*b*) What problem does this cause?

1

_____

* * * * *

Page four

Marks

13. (*a*) What was Jacques' childhood like? Mention any **one** thing.

1

_____

(*b*) What is his life like now? Mention any **one** thing.

1

_____

*   *   *   *   *

Total (25)

[*END OF QUESTION PAPER*]

[BLANK PAGE]

2008 | Credit

[BLANK PAGE]

Official SQA Past Papers: Credit French 2008

C

Total

1000/403

NATIONAL
QUALIFICATIONS
2008

TUESDAY, 13 MAY
11.10 AM – 12.10 PM

FRENCH
STANDARD GRADE
Credit Level
Reading

Fill in these boxes and read what is printed below.

Full name of centre

Town

Forename(s)

Surname

Date of birth
Day Month Year

Scottish candidate number

Number of seat

When you are told to do so, open your paper and write your answers **in English** in the spaces provided.

You may use a French dictionary.

Before leaving the examination room you must give this book to the invigilator. If you do not, you may lose all the marks for this paper.

Marks

1. You read an article in which some school pupils talk about friendships between boys and girls.

L'amitié filles—garçons

J'ai un petit copain, mais j'ai aussi beaucoup d'amis garçons. Quand j'ai des disputes avec mon copain, je peux parler à un autre garçon et cela m'aide à comprendre la mentalité masculine.

Valérie, 15 ans

Au collège, je fais partie d'une bande d'amis mixte. A la récréation nous sommes souvent ensemble et nous parlons de tout. Et nous faisons des sorties ensemble après les cours.

Thomas, 13 ans

Moi, je préfère discuter avec les filles individuellement. Elles rigolent tout le temps quand elles sont en groupe. Quand elles sont seules, par contre, on voit qu'elles ont leurs propres idées sur des sujets importants.

Marc, 15 ans

(*a*) What happens when Valérie has an argument with her boyfriend? Mention **two** things.

2

_____

_____

(*b*) What does Thomas say about his mixed group of friends? Mention any **two** things.

2

_____

_____

(*c*) Why does Marc prefer to speak to girls on an individual basis? Mention **two** things.

2

_____

_____

Marks

2. You then read one boy's ideas about how life might be in the future.

LA VIE DANS TRENTE ANS

La vie dans trente ans m'attire énormément car je pense que nous ne travaillerons plus. Tout le monde aura des robots qui feront notre boulot, bien sûr.

On se déplacera en voitures électriques ou bien je voyagerai en soucoupe volante dans l'espace et je parlerai avec des extra-terrestres qui seront, naturellement, mes meilleurs amis . . . Voilà.

Marc

(*a*) What does Marc say about work in 30 years time? Mention any **one** thing.

1

_____

(*b*) He goes on to describe a very different way of life in the future. What does he say? Mention any **two** things.

2

_____

_____

[Turn over

Marks

3. A girl then gives her ideas about the future.

> Mon rêve, c'est qu'en 2038 on aura trouvé des remèdes à tous les problèmes graves de nos jours. C'est-à-dire qu'il n'y aura plus de pauvreté ou de faim. Mais, à mon avis, ce n'est pas près d'arriver.
>
> Et voilà pourquoi. Je trouve que les gouvernements ne font pas assez pour résoudre les problèmes internationaux. Le pire c'est qu'ils préfèrent dépenser des sommes importantes sur les guerres alors que la moitié du monde meurt de faim.
>
> Thérèse

(a) What kind of world would Thérèse like to see in 2038? Mention any **one** thing.

1

_____

(b) Why does she think this is unlikely?

1

_____

(c) According to Thérèse, what are the worst things that governments do? Mention **two** things.

2

_____

_____

Marks

4. You then read an article about the work of a vet.

VÉTÉRINAIRE

Les vétérinaires s'intéressent bien sûr à la santé des animaux. Certains soignent des animaux domestiques. D'autres travaillent plutôt à la campagne en soignant les animaux de la ferme et d'autres encore s'occupent des animaux sauvages.

Certains vétérinaires font de la recherche en laboratoire, pour trouver des vaccins ou développer des médicaments. Leur travail profite ainsi à l'ensemble des animaux.

Ce qui est évident aussi, c'est qu'un vétérinaire doit aimer les animaux et avoir un très bon sens de l'observation. Un animal ne peut pas expliquer ce qu'il ressent et c'est au vétérinaire donc de savoir faire le diagnostic correct. En plus, il faut aussi être disponible vingt-quatre heures sur vingt-quatre parce que les "patients" peuvent tomber malades à tout moment.

(*a*) We are told that vets work with different groups of animals. Mention any **two** groups.

2

_____

_____

(*b*) What other type of work might a vet do? Mention any **one** thing.

1

_____

(*c*) Why is this type of work important?

1

_____

(*d*) Why does a vet require good powers of observation?

1

_____

(*e*) It takes commitment to be a vet. Explain why this is the case.

1

_____

[Turn over

Marks

DO NOT
WRITE IN
THIS
MARGIN

5. You read an article about Internet shopping in France.

15 millions de Français achètent en ligne

La France est le pays européen où les utilisateurs d'Internet adoptent le plus vite le commerce électronique.

Entre janvier et mars 2007, 15 millions de personnes ont fait un achat en ligne. C'est 2,5 millions de personnes de plus qu'en 2006. Pourquoi est-ce que les Français aiment de plus en plus acheter sur Internet?

Alors, d'abord c'est vite fait et on peut commander toutes sortes de marchandises sans quitter la maison et à n'importe quelle heure de la journée. Les sites de vente de personne à personne, comme par exemple Ebay, connaissent aussi un grand succès. Sur ces sites la plupart des gens sont honnêtes. Mais certains prennent l'argent pour un "objet vendu" et n'envoient jamais le produit.

Pour éviter ce problème, le gouvernement et les sites ont signé une Charte de Confiance. Ce document fixe des règles pour les échanges entre personnes sur les sites et protège le consommateur.

(a) How do recent figures show that French people have taken to Internet shopping? Mention **two** things.   **2**

_____

_____

(b) What are the advantages of buying online? Mention any **two** things.   **2**

_____

_____

(c) What problem can sometimes arise on the "person-to-person" sales sites?   **1**

_____

(d) What is the "Charter of Trust" intended to do? Mention **two** things.   **2**

_____

_____

Total (26)

[END OF QUESTION PAPER]

C

1000/409

NATIONAL
QUALIFICATIONS
2008

TUESDAY, 13 MAY
2.30 PM – 3.00 PM
(APPROX)

FRENCH
STANDARD GRADE
Credit Level
Listening Transcript

This paper must not be seen by any candidate.

The material overleaf is provided for use in an emergency only (eg the recording or equipment proving faulty) or where permission has been given in advance by SQA for the material to be read to candidates with additional support needs. The material must be read exactly as printed.

Transcript—Credit Level

> **Instructions to reader(s):**
>
> For each item, read the English **once,** then read the French **three times,** with an interval of 5 seconds between the readings. On completion of the third reading, pause for the length of time indicated in brackets after each item, to allow the candidates to write their answers.
>
> Where special arrangements have been agreed in advance to allow the reading of the material, those sections marked **(f)** should be read by a female speaker and those marked **(m)** by a male: those sections marked **(t)** should be read by the teacher.

(t) You are spending a holiday with your family at a campsite in France. One day, you meet André, a French boy who is also on holiday at the campsite.

(m) or (f) **Tu passes des vacances avec ta famille dans un camping en France. Un jour tu rencontres André, un jeune Français qui est aussi en vacances au camping.**

(t) **Question number one.**

André says he saw you at the campsite barbecue last night. Why did he not stay too late? Mention any **one** thing.

(m) **Je t'ai vu au barbecue hier soir. C'était génial, mais j'ai dû me coucher tôt parce que j'étais fatigué après le long voyage.**

(40 seconds)

(t) **Question number two.**

What does André say about his parents? What does he say about eating hamburgers? Mention **two** things.

(m) **A la maison, mes parents sont assez stricts. Je peux manger des hamburgers seulement une fois par semaine. Normalement, je vais au fast-food le vendredi soir avec mes copains.**

(40 seconds)

(t) **Question number three.**

What rules do André's parents have if he goes out during the week? Mention any **one** thing.

(m) **Si je sors dans la semaine je dois rentrer à onze heures et, bien sûr, je dois finir mes devoirs avant de sortir.**

(40 seconds)

(t) **Question number four.**

What does he say about weekends? Mention any **one** thing.

(m) **Le week-end j'ai un peu plus de liberté. Pourtant, je ne vais pas au centre-ville parce que c'est trop dangereux.**

(40 seconds)

(t) André's family is concerned about the environment.

Question number five.

What does André's father do to protect the environment? Mention any **one** thing.

How else does the family help the environment?

(m) **Tous les jours mon père va au travail en vélo. En général, il utilise la voiture seulement le week-end.**

En plus, chez nous, nous avons trois poubelles, la poubelle normale et deux autres—une pour les papiers et une pour les bouteilles.

(40 seconds)

(t) **Question number six.**

André's father is a reporter on the local newspaper.

How does André help him at weekends? Mention **two** things.

(m) **Mon père est reporter pour le journal de notre ville. Le week-end, je fais des recherches pour lui sur Internet et je téléphone aux gens pour organiser des interviews.**

(40 seconds)

(t) **Question number seven.**

Why does André like doing this work? Mention **two** things.

(m) **C'est bien, parce que je gagne de l'argent de poche et quelquefois je rencontre des personnes importantes.**

(40 seconds)

(t) One evening you hear a radio interview with Sophie Corbin who became famous after winning a singing competition on television.

Question number eight.

Sophie talks about her love of music. What does she say?

(f) **La musique me passionne. A l'âge de cinq ou six ans, j'ai décidé que je voulais devenir chanteuse professionnelle.**

(40 seconds)

(t) **Question number nine.**

In what way was Sophie supported at home? Mention **two** things.

(f) **Mes parents m'ont encouragée tous les deux et c'est ma mère qui m'emmenait aux cours de danse et de musique.**

(40 seconds)

[Turn over for Questions 10 to 14 on *Page four*

(t)   Question number ten.

Sophie has a busy lifestyle now. How does she try to stay healthy? Mention any **three** things.

(f)   Ma vie est très chargée et pour rester en forme j'ai quatre règles. D'abord, il me faut huit heures de sommeil chaque nuit et en plus je mange équilibré. Pour une chanteuse il est nécessaire de protéger sa voix. Donc, je ne fume pas et je bois trois litres d'eau par jour.

(40 seconds)

(t)   Question number eleven.

In what way has Sophie's life changed since she won the competition? Mention any **two** things.

(f)   Ma vie a complètement changé. Je n'ai plus de problèmes financiers; alors, je porte des vêtements de marque et je loge dans des hôtels de luxe, des hôtels cinq étoiles.

(40 seconds)

(t)   Question number twelve.

She mentions some disadvantages. What does she say? Mention any **two** things.

(f)   Mais il y a aussi des aspects négatifs . . . par exemple, je n'ai pas beaucoup de temps libre, mes amis me manquent énormément et je ne vois pas souvent mes parents.

(40 seconds)

(t)   Question number thirteen.

Sophie considers herself to be lucky. What does she say? Mention **two** things.

(f)   J'ai eu de la chance car j'ai déjà visité plusieurs pays et j'ai fait des concerts avec des chanteurs très célèbres.

(40 seconds)

(t)   Question number fourteen.

Sophie goes on to talk about the future. What does she say? Mention any **one** thing.

(f)   Pour le moment je suis très populaire mais on ne sait jamais si ça va durer longtemps. Beaucoup de jeunes voudraient prendre ma place dans l'avenir.

(40 seconds)

(t)   End of test.

Now look over your answers.

[END OF TRANSCRIPT]

C

FOR OFFICIAL USE

Total Marks

1000/408

NATIONAL
QUALIFICATIONS
2008

TUESDAY, 13 MAY
2.30 PM – 3.00 PM
(APPROX)

FRENCH
STANDARD GRADE
Credit Level
Listening

Fill in these boxes and read what is printed below.

Full name of centre

Town

Forename(s)

Surname

Date of birth
Day Month Year   Scottish candidate number   Number of seat

When you are told to do so, open your paper.

You will hear a number of short items in French. You will hear each item three times, then you will have time to write your answer.

Write your answers, **in English**, in this book, in the appropriate spaces.

You may take notes as you are listening to the French, but only in this book.

You may **not** use a French dictionary.

You are not allowed to leave the examination room until the end of the test.

Before leaving the examination room you must give this book to the invigilator. If you do not, you may lose all the marks for this paper.

Marks

You are spending a holiday with your family at a campsite in France. One day, you meet André, a French boy who is also on holiday at the campsite.

Tu passes des vacances avec ta famille dans un camping en France. Un jour tu rencontres André, un jeune Français qui est aussi en vacances au camping.

1. André says he saw you at the campsite barbecue last night. Why did he not stay too late? Mention any **one** thing.

1

_____

*   *   *   *   *

2. (*a*)   What does André say about his parents?

1

_____

(*b*)   What does he say about eating hamburgers? Mention **two** things.

2

_____

_____

*   *   *   *   *

3. What rules do André's parents have if he goes out during the week? Mention any **one** thing.

1

_____

*   *   *   *   *

4. What does he say about weekends? Mention any **one** thing.

1

_____

*   *   *   *   *

André's family is concerned about the environment.

5. (*a*)   What does André's father do to protect the environment? Mention any **one** thing.

1

_____

(*b*)   How else does the family help the environment?

1

_____

*   *   *   *   *

Marks

6. André's father is a reporter on the local newspaper. How does André help him at weekends? Mention **two** things.

2

_____

_____

*   *   *   *   *

7. Why does André like doing this work? Mention **two** things.

2

_____

_____

*   *   *   *   *

One evening you hear a radio interview with Sophie Corbin who became famous after winning a singing competition on television.

8. Sophie talks about her love of music. What does she say?

1

_____

*   *   *   *   *

9. In what way was Sophie supported at home? Mention **two** things.

2

_____

_____

*   *   *   *   *

10. Sophie has a busy lifestyle now. How does she try to stay healthy? Mention any **three** things.

3

_____

_____

_____

*   *   *   *   *

[Turn over for Questions 11 to 14 on *Page four*

Marks

11. In what way has Sophie's life changed since she won the competition? Mention any **two** things.

2

_____

_____

* * * * *

12. She mentions some disadvantages. What does she say? Mention any **two** things.

2

_____

_____

* * * * *

13. Sophie considers herself to be lucky. What does she say? Mention **two** things.

2

_____

_____

* * * * *

14. Sophie goes on to talk about the future. What does she say? Mention any **one** thing.

1

_____

* * * * *

Total (25)

[END OF QUESTION PAPER]

[BLANK PAGE]

[BLANK PAGE]

[BLANK PAGE]

[BLANK PAGE]

[BLANK PAGE]

[BLANK PAGE]